the black body with Love, stardust

Naomi Jones

contents

Stardust (n.)

(not in technical use) a mass of distant stars appearing as tiny particles of
dust.

'though not the dust we're used to. always in a head nod - a look in syntax
across the room - a southern twang-
it's what we see in an infant's eyes. the way we play with dolphin backs, in
'pats of brotherhood- a familiarity.

a naively romantic quality:

that always remembers the silence between us is never figurative and quite
frankly never heard.
The fantasí.

heart without a soul[1]

To forget existence is possible without her hands, is to forget my origins
My grandmother's hands would lift me out of wrinkled bed sheets in the mornings.

I realized it wasn't possible to move and manufacture peace inside fallacies
her truth around her waist, beaded between not black enough 'nd not latina either.

When exes dispose of astral bodies 'cause they're possessed and displaced
her stomach folds exist on their own planes, they follow, bellow and procreate.

Trauma is felt in each separate body until all are in complete contagion
all her beauty scabs her belly from razors trying to adjust and override S.O.P

Complete disarray.
Total reset.

---

[1] "Not to know what happened before you were born is to remain forever a child." -CICERO
"No man can know where he is going unless he knows exactly where he has been and exactly how he arrived at his present place." -MAYA ANGELOU

"Most of us think of trauma as something that occurs in an individual body, like a toothache or a broken arm. But trauma also routinely spreads between bodies, like a contagious disease. When someone with unhealed trauma chooses dirty pain over clean pain, the person may try to soothe his or her trauma by blowing it through another person—using violence, rage, coercion, deception, betrayal, or emotional abuse. This never heals the trauma. Instead, it increases the first person's dirty pain by reinforcing harmful and aggressive survival strategies as standard operating procedure. It creates a sense of ongoing unease in the first person's body that he or she then must override. It may also provoke a reflexively defensive or aggressive response in the second person's body" (Menakem *My Grandmother's Hands* 54).

body without weight

She walks with the moon,
a kind of waltz with its craters
that never seems dangerous
for a deity in this universe.
Until
her curiosity ran with the giants of consciousness,
the communal, the collective if
-- then.
Then she glances, making connection
with dirts and sands and dust
No atmosphere but she,
rooted amidst befores and afters, she
reflecting on the identity within each
refracting glare, she
Daring the sun to flicker[2]
before she shines; she

                        moves on.

---

[2] A nod towards Porsha Olayiwola's "Parable" piece, "daring the star to flicker before I get to shine… the stars blow themselves up"

hello morning

waking up to despair
is the hardest
it feels like the nightmares'
white frame followed you
Here
and i wish i could write these words more carefully
the margins of my paperless thoughts are sun rays
they show you exactly where my thoughts would be
if they were as weightless as my heart in the morning.

dear marigolds

do you find yourself
in teardrops or in sorrow

when in copper sequins
refract from the iris in
your face you grow
you bend in splash and
ripple you coexist in creations first step

You-
find the moon is your only lover
and ask for more time
with its holes maybe this night
you can plug the memory of sorrow

do you want happiness or peace?

scale of breathing

What is the scale of breathing
When it's lodged between each lung—
Is it cacophonous in there?
Like is there Control and chaos simultaneously
A dissonance or a harmony?
A synapse of when heart and mind
Sew soul to muscle with cages of bone—

How is it possible that standing here
Right now, I feel the past and future
Ancestral breath as one
I am in love with my ancestors' dreams of me
In love with these future moments, yet still weary
of their present tap on my shoulder.

I want to know what it's like
to hear your breath in the wind
both constant and inconsistent.
Will It pass through me and this body
with the next? I understand our time is so relatively cyclical it holds you
and I in the same place
feeling similar things
Knowing nothing of everything and everything of nothing.

For once I can smell the joy in the grass blades,
be able to breathe in the scent of the clouds
as they pass overhead. I understand that this place
where I stand is no longer constant

But rather a memory
Of me and stage and body
Of me and body and soul
Of me and my friends and everything that I have to let go of

You've taught me how to say goodbye but I'm not sure I want to.
I am thankful for the chaos and the changes
The glow ups and let downs
The trial and the error
The overcompensated the ugliness
The beauty

I am my ancestors wildest dreams
And for their dreams I shall live for these moments
I can dream my next generations will flourish
in the roots I plant for them.
Generational breath, survival, existence--
eternal.

lungs

some nights i wake up most like my father,
wiry-eyed and passionate about the things outside of my control
I didn't exist but for the use of others.
>   *the Daddy fix it(s)*
>   I don't usually tell this story.[3]
but something about these lungs trapped in this cage makes sense
as a comparison between black man and black body.
both are stuck behind bars-- both, like my muscles, are in need of breath
>   see I don't usually tell this story,
But something about it just seems so familiar;
The weight of the fabrics make sense between my fingers
I am currently and previously in love with the scent
>   *I cannot prove anything about this tale,*
>   *Yet the feeble fables be merry in it's presence.*
I am a multitude of here and there, and feeling with uplifting
>   But most times I refuse to tell this story
Because to most it won't make sense.
I should not have survived with everything
when everything is trying to kill me.
>   *Ancestral breath kept me alive,*
>   *when locating and breathing in stardust*
I incongruently measured the angles to happiness
Through the warmth in another man's arms
when all I needed was my Father.
>   I don't usually like to tell this story.
Because people get confused on where it comes from.
Where my anger originates, forgetting the all important factor

---

[3] A nod to the structural set up of "Parable" by Porsha Olayiwola from *I Shimmer Sometimes, Too.*

that it is not solely mine, but that of a people before the age of Capricorns.
I hate telling this story.
because they might mistake my multi-tude, my intersection,
my story is as ripple is to wave. A moment
in a history of outcries, this cry mentions only one name.

rain

I envy the rain.
Unironically.
It leaps to an unknown cadence and never fumbles.

a conjunction of molecules forming a connection
with all the components that keep me alive.

I used to try and set it on fire.
Ironically
It never worked. It only boiled--

Compared the sizzling feeling of this
wet component on my black-top skin.

Some nights the stars set themselves on fire,
just so we may repeat the cadence of the burns.
Ever notice how people will admire the raindance,
Just as much as the fire's.

Both reflecting some sort of energy interlaced in their bodies. Their masses
holding power, but never the ignition. Holding the trigger, but never the
safety pin. Holding the belly,

                                          but never the baby.[4]

---

[4] "so two black boys and the eyes of small islands, the hands of striving fathers, the dying
hands of legends. and all the smarts in the world and their stinging and their singing
against the sharpest piece of air. and the years of decisions while they make all their
choices and have all their children and lose all their hair. and their one prep school and
their one university full of white boy legacy and dark shared knowing. and worlds of
belonging turned longing and loss. universe of belonging turned longing and loss. and two

mem'ry

I am power
It folds in my veins and bloodstream,
It intermingled with my blood cells
It sprinted through my heart
Into my medulla oblongata
Came out in my actions
In my walk
In my creative outlets
Whispered in the spaces left on this page[5]
Screamed in the static uprising
from my sweat out edges

<hr>

black boys with each other at least. with each other at most" (Alexis Pauline Gums *DUB* 133).

[5] "what happens when you are forced to endure something you can't bear to remember. what happens when the only way to endure is by not remembering. what happens when one day remembering becomes the only way to survive. the good news is he is still alive. and cousins come by and visit sometimes" (Alexis Pauline Gumbs *Dub: Finding Ceremony* 118).

have you chosen your body?

I know I deserve love but am I making it too hard by forcing people that I truly love to work for it? Wait for it. I think the best version of what I want is a reflection of how deeply I love. Is it impossible to reflect and desire and deserve love in the way that I give it? Is it ignorant? I assumed this position of being Black and woman and writer and poet and voice and human to be easy. Perhaps because my mother made it look as such. Perhaps because I never saw the dangers and the risks, as brought about and as lived in my grandmothers' bodies and their mothers' souls. Perhaps it's because struggle does not exist for those nearest to me in the way the world describes it for Black women. Maybe I just don't see my own struggle as I constantly invalidate it. I have a lot of questions and no answers. I have to learn to unwrap myself from the hug of gravity and understand that I cannot be an earth bound soul. Because the only thing that holds me here is a worldly understanding that I cannot be up there with my ancestors in the stars and here at the same time. the stars themselves see like angels, they can fly because they learned to take themselves as air. Maybe I am just stuck in this learning phase of unlearning gravity.

eve?

Genisis 3:19

It started with a confused boy horny for

chapel sex in rebellion of the church. No part of us is digestible

      rather it straddles black thigh in church pews

      to explain the right thing to do

to behave in obedience and make no mistake you were

an afterthought. Sand drizzled in a naïve womb too desolate[6]

      straddle an open black mouth hungry for attention

      for an explanation for your story.

I'd rather not apologize for keeping you. I'd remember your face if

I aborted you, so I birthed in isolation outside of a hospital room.

      your father's straddle unlearned waist, all too slow

      to expect us to reason with his abusive history.

Every beat on the monitor meant you were alive, and I had to protect

you, son, for our mediocre survival was pieced together with scotch tape.

In the sweat of thy face shalt thou eat bread till thou return unto the ground

From the scraps of cereal made into meals,

to the welfare checks that paid nothing but the light bill.

      you know creation straddles my black thigh and

      black throat until my sorrow was written in ghost stories

---

[6] "i knew touch and i knew truth. i knew age and i knew youth. i knew tenderness and proof. i didn't show it though. i knew bit lips to wait. i knew you wouldn't be too late. i knew the half was not our fate. i knew the game." (Alexis Pauline Gumbs *Dub* 35).

on my pillow. From tithes that became your college fund while 'extra'

paid for formula, for scrapped knees, for fevers, for food to

            an unforgiving straddle on my guilty black thigh making

            ends meet with the unexplained cum stains in my story.

From the check-out lines in your favorite grocery store where

I had to explain that we couldn't buy blankets on food stamps;

            to your pout and stammering on thigh strangled for

            a better explanation or excuse for 'ends meet' stories.

how can I explain that we made it only through miracles and

donation piles and unemployment checks and unopened prayers

for out of it wast thou taken; for dust thou art, and unto dust shalt thou return.

what is this war?

 I thought I was in love twice.
And for different reasons both survived.
One was intellect. A strong desire for what my ears could see.
The way words toyed with music scores,
balanced indignity with humility,
but ran pride through tire tracks
watched it choose to run
And somehow -- We remain

The other I do not try to understand.
it holds no weight for gravitational attraction
rather the thrust of each wave is crash into the bellows
rather sweep the sand the help that unsettles the sleeping nests
and it makes no sense.

yet still in all ways it remains.

what's in meanings if love doesn't --

I breathe between the lengths of your smile.

Every time you open your mouth

The world falls to a hush.

You command attention, but

Less aggressively, I guess I am in love with you.

Have you seen the way the clouds will part for you?

Have they not known your undeniable strength?

From Love.

no hay vergüenza

hug my hills

pretending to sleep in the

backseat while he drums

forehead kisses while the

orchestra symphonic collapse

catharsis in each dissonant maj. 7 chord

they are the release of joy

like angles written in black lines

comfort my ancestry comes from

I know the world would like me to believe.

Black boy who dies Black

Black
I.
I'm scared to have a black baby
I know that what comes from this womb
is prejudged as curse before it kicks
Before it form inside their first home the wall will swallow it to protect it
Before it's body transforms from zygote to fetus, it's death date it chosen
Before it's hands develop
Before it's eyes open

I know that before they take their first step
They must learn to stand
They will hold my hand with their brown fingers
They will squeeze at my neck when learning to
climb, to pull to stand, to raise both hands.

They will be more of me than I am,
But I'm scared they will learn too quickly what
Words to be afraid of
I am scared that I must teach them that not all cops and not all whites
and not all systems, while, they live within the oppression of one.

I am scared they will know what the barrel of a gun looks like
In sun and at night before they know
What fireflies are
I'm scared their hands will plug bullet holes
Before they pluck at boogers

I worry that my baby won't know how to say daddy

But will remember to restate their name and
where they live and their mothers cell phone number
before they ask if they can breathe

I'm scared they will learn how to hold their
breath as to protect their life from someone
Not thinking
Or seeing
That they are my baby[7]
That they are human
That their skin their ethnicity their culture aren't potential criminals

I'm worried all my womb can produce is targets
The bullseye of their heart beat ticking to the drum of stop resisting
I fear the day their frustration is misunderstood for threatening behavior
Their run route is mistaken for a criminal escape
Their home is broken into by off duty cops and their defense is bullet holes
They knock on the wrong door and mistaken for a forced entry
That Their deposit doesn't go through when they thought and they write a
check too early
That their name is more Divine when written twice
Birth and death date

I'm worried that I will live past them,
So if I tell you that I am okay
it's probably a cover up for the immense anxiety I feel to bring a child

---

[7] "I've heard sharks followed slave ships crossing the Atlantic Ocean trailing black bodies
thrown overboard… i heard come hell or high water, they were going to watch n*ggas
drown in a hurricane down south. I heard they knew the levees was going to give in and
break, knew the waters was coming to wash n*ggas away. Tell me, how do a n*gga keep
their head above water if n*ggas can't swim? … N*ggas jump, but never jump in, I sprint,
you swim. N*ggas can't float, our bodies too dense" (Porsha Olayiwola "Water").

Into this world and see their end
On the 10 o clock news.

blues

don't forget to breathe.

reds

I've seen my mind could paint a thousand pictures

Dust it off take out the lens and see a blurred picture

Hold it back and let the paint brush be my intermission

But i guess i'm just another poet in the vision

Say I'm

Scripting visions on an underline

italicize

the verbalized

voices on the inside

Unprophicized[8]

Yea They were silenced by the white skin

The body thin

The makeup always done to a 10

Now back then

I was Illusive towards eternity

Knit into reality

Understand my inner-workings were never a fallacy

I devised a simple plan that would change reality

____

[8] Undoing the false prophecies from false prophets

So prose could listen to the fate inside their history-unraveling peace

she looks at her emotions independently

never allowing them to touch.

       to become as round as she

excusing their brashness, falling deeper

into the membranes lodges in echolocated fat[9]

she finds her dreams have the same setting.

       as free flowing as a ripple

directed, coordinated wave length.

she replicates this sound across decades.

her generations hearing this warcry.

this outcry for peace everlasting.

           its no wonder the black body can survive despite.

          it defies the odds because of an ancestral beckoning.

        a call and response once started at the birth of ish and isha.

       i grew roots in places i didn't know i needed to be grounded in.

         it began as time forced everything to end.

---

[9] "Echolocation and communication overlap but they also diverge. Sometimes the sounds I make are about measuring my surroundings. Sometimes there is something I need to tell you. Usually it's both. Dolphins use the fat in their foreheads to modulate their biosonar listening, which sounds about as elegant as what I do with you. Sometimes I feel like I'm communicating with you underwater. The impact of what I say outlives what I learned by saying it." (Alexis Pauline Gumbs *Undrowned* 13).

so we grieve the same prayer for peace.

we sing the melodies of sorrow as harmonic folk songs.

we create. we destroy. we build. we riot. We dream.

and if creation reveals itself to be human, it will not

recognize us.

it will ask the Body what has become of its ligaments

and never reveal the disappointment for our

collective corpses.

warp this body

Interlace my fingers with yours
[10]Placed in air is pride
Under the covers is love
Out in public is taboo

I... in you...

What is love but a figurative choice?
Have you chosen me today?

----

[10] "remember when we met? underwater weightless and flowering. remember when we
laced fingers or didn't based on tides or passing whales. remember how our breathing
turned into what would support us and everything else in the thousand-mile radius of
echo. and how our heartbeats were no different than this ocean pulled by moon?5" (Alexis
Pauline Gumbs *M Archive* 111).

notice

"the world looks different when the sun is gone." -Jamie L. Woods

how frank to notice
we live between two stars
and 100 billion galaxies—

and we worry about one
— sun.

mem'ry

Mommy what's it like when you fall in love
What's it like to be kissed between the raindrops as they fall
Is there such thing as glee when sorrow must also co exist
How do we forget how to love someone to better ourselves for the time
being.
>   you must remember the sound of the rain
>   it only counts minuets in 100ths
>   in here it remembers to communicate with the earth
>   it recalls the depth of an oath and floats on it's back
>   *love can only exist in the mem'ry of what it once was*
Is it a fairytale?
Does it understand princesses like us don't get prince charming just
the dust of what one? Is there ever a moment of weakness?
Can it tell the difference between it and lust?
What aren't you telling me about love?
>   how should i explain a phenomenon?
>   a gift given to us by Love themself on the journey to
>   mem'ry of why they chose man in the first place? There is always
>   competition. only you choose the difference,
>   You are the only thing it requires.
>   *i doubt it recalls the struggle to love without hate*[11]
>   *The heat in passion and the journey in sorrow.*
>   *Love is all of these things in emotional rollercoasters.*
>   *But you go through it for the sake of love.*

---

[11] "her mother is the warning that said use your brain to protect your heart. her mother is not that dark place she doesn't remember… mother is the name of the one who can save you. mother is the name of the one who comes when you scream. mother is the name of the one who keeps you warm. where were you when the sun died?" (Gumbs *M Archive* 123-124).

figurines

The Brown body stands at the front display case;
left in-between the drawn curtain
and the vacant gray sidewalks.
A sale sign hung above her.

A mannequin surrounded in red silk
lit by the overhead white light like
it's dancing among the curves and ripples
of this brown-skin,
wrapped around the arms and legs and hips and thighs
and breasts the texture of sea glass.[12]

The brown husk like diamonds
against a fluorescent white spotlight,
Brown Body like camera and lens;
catch the satin insteps that hold her in a cloud, the store
uses her as marketing tactic: ever wonder
if she squints to see her audience

---

[12] "her mother is not Africa. Africa is the place where she swam in the dark. no. Africa is
the place before she screamed chained there in the dark. her memory of her mother is the
truth that taught her shallower breaths would save her in that cold place that wet place
where ever after it hurt to breathe" (Alexis Pauline Gumbs *M Archive* 123).

beyond survival

I am but a mere comprehension
         of what this world could be.
         But I only comprehend
            very little [13]
         of what <u>truly</u> affects me so I guess in that way
        I'm self-centered-selfish even
        because I risk understanding love
      for the purpose of entertaining the idea of purity

one that does not exist.

     I think I ignore these concepts

         for the comfort of worldliness
       of being accepted and praised and regarded
           and appreciated but then i realize
this world is a prayer closet of which i am not supposed to get the glory
        yet give it.

---

[13] "The lies of adolescence and young adulthood are formative and legion. Here is where we either begin the journey towards consciousness or retreat into a lifetime of waking sleep. The lies of young adulthood circle issues of identity and agency and meaning. Where do I belong in the scheme of things? Why do I have, or not have, the things I have or do not have? How much of what I've been taught is true? What do I deserve from this world? What am I obligated to give? We answer these questions, and if we lie we set the foundation for bigger, more desperate lies. We pass from innocence into self-delusion, from the world of not knowing to the world of refusing to know" (Kim Mclarin 82).

open

I want to tell you a love story

How ink and page first met.

she wants to be here as open as the first

sight of fire to air. she wants your breath

but is scared to ask for all that gives you life.

She wanted your hand, not for touch or

support but to inquire

what the hand of God looked like,

when he said, 'let it be beautiful'

ink was a lonely discovery only remembered

by those focused on its enriched

thick appearance. It played with burnt candle

wicks and kissed blankets of sut.

it wore a glimmer when it met page

so ready for its imprint

so lifeless without its flare

and spill and mistake. they learned

each other. Focused first on body

on how their 2 dimensional love

would reach through its full page.

yearning for forgiveness, learning

what an open book will look like.

exist

Black people let's write you a love letter,[14]
For the way you never dim, always vibrant,
Laughing.
Exploding.

Let's let you experience joy and water
For the width of an ocean and the depth of
release
Pressure.

Let's cause an earthquake with your laugh
bring pangea to its roots through the bellows
The wheezes
The knee cap slaps.

Let's let them see your roots in sun flares
And garden your wildberries,
And guard your bodies.

Let's let you live.

---

[14] "I am with you. And I love your wise audacious boundaries. I love your visible evolution.
I love your decadent adaptation in a world of watered mouths. I love your bristle and your
backbone. The way you breathe through your whole body. The way you can freeze
onlookers with your eyes and build worlds out of edge and frost and melt. You work of art.
You magic bell. You jar of genius. Map of galaxies. You goad the world to roughen texture.
Tempt the sky to fall in rings" (Alexis Pauline Gumbs *Undrowned* 74).

in stardust

Beautiful beautiful
Beautiful black girl
let the crowds gawk at your prowess
your skin that swallows the sun's rays
your hair created the atmosphere.

men will compete for your water
and fierce and design, you
will be torn for the gems that
whisper through your sheath
while hurt, you must look to heal,
remember.

Hurt men cannot love you.
Beautiful black people- hurt men cannot love you.
Hurt man does not love.

Remember the paint that makes up your existence is
regardless of those who attack
Our survival
our strength
us being loved
or cherished.
there are some who resent us

who'd rather see us broken and down and submissive
And yet feel the pain before we understand where it's coming from.
We feel their pain. We look at their words and feel their pain
and I need you to know, my beautiful empath

that hurt people cannot love you.
That they will look you in the eye and use you
until you're completely barren and then cast you aside.

Do not be a doormat my beautiful empath,
for you are the lightbulb
you are the ever changing
ever consistent plug
you are the electricity
the lighting bolt
the shore bed
the ocean
you are the beauty and you are the mischief

I appreciate you for the way you try to never judge a human
before they ever walk in the door. to never judge a situation
based off of its title, but please know
not every space is meant for your energy

my beautiful empath your emotions are more 360
on every single hour than any person that will pass you on the street.
you have an understanding of frequencies that is unmatched.
you have incomparable beauty
you have intelligence and mindfulness and softness
but strength and hardness and bullet proof toughness you

my beautiful empath, are perfect beyond purity
no matter how many mistakes you have made
you are precisely the exact thing that deserves praise and reprise
a chorus and a verse
a song written after how deeply you feel everyone else's frequency

you are rhythmically advanced.

remember,
hurt people cannot love you
recall
hurt people cannot love you
comprehend
that hurt people cannot love you.

Repeat. I am stardust, I am stardust, I am love and infinite immortality,
I am cyclical and breath and ocean and ripple
I am petal and leaf and wind and sunshine and raindrops and angelic.
I will promise to heal myself before I love you.

in conversation with

Gumbs, Alexis Pauline. *Dub: Finding Ceremony.* Duke University Press, 2020.

Gumbs, Alexis Pauline. *M Archive: After the End of the World.* Duke University Press, 2018.

Gumbs, Alexis Pauline. *Undrowned.* AK Press, 2021.

McLarin, Kim. *Womanish: a Grown Black Woman Speaks on Love and Life.* Ig Publishing, 2019.

Menakem, Resmaa. *My Grandmother's Hands: My grandmother's hands: racialized trauma and the*
pathway to mending our hearts and bodies. Penguin Press, 2021.

Olayiwola, Porsha. "Parable." and "Water." *I Shimmer Sometimes, Too.* Button Poetry, 2019.

Notes on Pleasure activism from adrienne maree brown's podcast Octavia Tried to Tell Us.